For our wild animals

Written by: Nathan Dye
Illustrated by: Chris Dye

Memphis is a leopard. She's recently moved north with her family.

Memphis was very excited about her new home.

Fact: Leopards are exceptional climbers and enjoy taking rests in the high branches of trees during the day.

On her first day at her new school,
Memphis could feel everyone looking at her.
Most of the kids had never even seen a leopard
before. They thought she was a cheetah.

Fact: Most leopards are light colored and have dark spots on their fur called "rosettes" that resemble the shape of a rose. Cheetahs have a clear, single, black spot separated from the other spots on the cat's body.

"Oooh look at that cheetah,
I hear they're really fast,"
said Hudson the bunny.

Fact: Leopards are very solitary and spend most of their time alone.

Memphis was too shy to correct them
because she didn't want to seem rude.

She just wanted people to like her.

So, she just let them all go on
believing she was a cheetah.

After settling in, Memphis was really loving school, her new friends and all of her classes.

But deep down, she knew she was not totally being herself.

One day, the track coach came to their class to talk about the spring meet.

All the animals got excited knowing they'd win with a cheetah on their team.

Fact: The cheetah is the fastest land animal in the world, reaching speeds of up to 70 miles per hour. Leopards only reach a top speed of about 37 miles per hour.

Memphis knew she was in trouble.

When everyone found out she wasn't who she was pretending to be, she just knew they wouldn't be friends with her anymore.

The next morning, Memphis told her mom she was too sick to go to school, but her mom wasn't falling for it.

Fact: Female leopards are excellent mothers. They have a gestation period of 3 months and can give birth to two or three cubs.

Memphis told her mom what had happened, and how she didn't exactly lie about being a cheetah, she just didn't correct everyone when they thought she was one.

Her mother understood why she wanted so badly to make friends, but explained that if she wasn't being true to herself,

On her way into school that day, Memphis met with her friend Lucy and told her the truth – that she wasn't a cheetah.

Instead of being mad, Lucy surprised Memphis with a huge hug.

Fact: The Eurasian lynx is Europe's third largest predator; its body is short and it has long legs with large feet. Its ears have a distinctive black tuft at its tip and its paws have retractile sharp claws.

That day before the meet,
Memphis told her team that she was really a leopard.

She was very scared, but relieved at the same time –
it felt good to let the truth out.

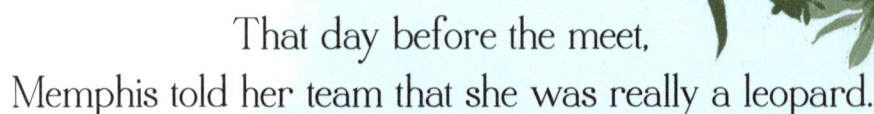

Fact: Leopards can be found in various places around the world – they live in
Sub-Saharan Africa, northeast Africa, Central Asia, India and China.

# LEOPARD or CHEETAH

### BY MEMPHIS THE LEOPARD

**LEOPARDS ARE:**
1. FAST
2. GOOD SWIMMER
3. GOOD CLIMBER
4. COVERED WITH "ROSETTES"

**CHEETAHS ARE:**
1. REALLY FAST
2. I MEAN SO FAST!!!
3. FAAAAAST!
4. COVERED WITH SPOTS

Much to her surprise, her friends laughed and gave her a huge hug, and told her she should maybe just enter the long jump.

They told her they weren't friends with her because of her spots, they liked her for her.

This is a story about being true to yourself.

You can't change your spots, so you should always be who you are.

Fact: Leopards love to climb and can even carry heavy loads up into the tree with them.

www.ingramcontent.com/pod-product-compliance
Lightning Source LLC
Chambersburg PA
CBHW062024290426
44108CB00024B/2767